Loss Prevention: Catch a Shoplifter

ROHULLAH LATIF

HADIA BHAROOCHA

OMAR BANUELOS

ISBN: 1515304213
ISBN-13: 978-1515304210

CONTENTS

ACKNOWLEDGMENTS

This book is to act as a quick reference guide to Loss Prevention. We had been fortunate enough to have great mentors in our career and we only hope you share what we have learned through our experiences. Enjoy!

1 WHAT IS LOSS PREVENTION

Imagine walking into your local store, you're in line paying for your merchandise and suddenly notice two individuals running towards an exit of the store. You then witness the same two individuals walking back into the store with a third subject and disappear into a secluded office. Congratulations! Whether you realized it or not, you just had your first interaction with Loss Prevention.

Over the years, shoplifting has become a career choice for many. There are people who wake up in the morning and have the intention to cause a loss to a company for their own gain. As shoplifting has increased, so has the demand for Loss Prevention Agents. Pursuing a career in Loss Prevention can be extremely rewarding. In this field, opportunities to grow and develop can be achieved fairly easy in little time with hard work and dedication.

The demand for Loss Prevention Agents is increasing at a high rate. More and more companies are realizing that their profits are plummeting due to lack of Loss

Prevention. Major companies such as Sears, Target, Kohl's, Macy's, CVS, Walmart, etc. all have a Loss Prevention team protecting their assets. With this surge in the demand for Loss Prevention Agents, there has also been a higher demand of QUALITY agents with EXPERIENCE & KNOWLEDGE. This is where you come into play! We welcome you to a very challenging yet rewarding career!

Loss Prevention can be broken down into five different categories, we like to call it SIPE!

Safety: Safety is not just the right thing to focus on but it is also the most costly piece to any company! An average shoplifter will get away with around $80 worth of merchandise on a good day, but one injury can cost around $400 for just the first clinic visit!

Internals: Internals or internal is something that the Loss Prevention Manager focuses on. Employees regularly cause loss to the company many different ways and it is the responsibility of the Loss Prevention Manager to find out whether the loss was caused due to honest mistakes or dishonest intentions.

People: Always remember, that at the end of the day, shortage is everyone's game. Establish strong partnerships with people. Partner with local law enforcement to gain support, create strong loss prevention cultures within the store. Have everyone play!

Externals: Externals or external theft is considered the

bread and butter of loss prevention. Catching shoplifters while may be fun and rewarding, is by no stretch of the imagination an easy task. Apprehending shoplifters not only prevents shortage on the given day but can prevent theft from occurring in the future.

Shrink: Shrink or Shortage is the loss a company sustains over the given year, this number is calculated in $'s lost over annual sales to get a Shrink %. The magic rule in retail is to always aim for 1% or under.

Knowledge of the SIPES will greatly increase your chances of catching a shoplifter.

2 SAFETY
"Protect Thy Loved Ones"

Safety is one of the most important aspects in Loss Prevention. Both, safety for customers as well as associates helps minimize a company's loss. It can affect your stores dollars in both General Liability and Workers' Compensation.

Safety Hazards can be can be categorized into two separate categories.

1. Physical: ex. spills, trips, falls.

2. Behavioral: ex. associate behavior & tendencies, safety ethics

Responding to Physical Safety Hazards

> Spills: Spill Kits should be readily available in designated areas in store.

> ➤ Taking the right steps when responding to a spill is crucial.

Step 1: Identify and do not walk away
Step 2: Contain spill & caution
Step 3: Re-route foot traffic
Step 4: Clean/verify area

Slips, Trips, & Falls (STP):

Assessing the store prior to opening and also during operating hours for STF Hazards can greatly decrease associate/customer accidents. Responding to a STF Hazards in a timely manner, if not immediately, can be the difference between having an associate/customer accident vs. not having one at all.

Never walk by! Fix any STF hazards on the spot. Remember, safety is more important than theft and should be treated that way. In the event that something cannot be fixed immediately, make sure to make it inaccessible to customers and employees and come back to it immediately.

Personal Protective Equipment

Protective Equipment provided to prevent any injuries while on the job.

There are 5 things that can be considered Personal Protective Equipment
1) Gloves
2) Goggles
3) Sheathed Box Cutters
4) Back Braces
5) Face Masks

Safety Behaviors and Ethics

Safety Behaviors can be displayed by associates and will be identified when you're present. Safety Ethics are not visible and are displayed by associates when they believe that they are alone and out of sight.

Safety Behavior
> Wearing back-belts but not strapping on properly
> Placing merchandise on floor when adjusting displays
> Improper lifting techniques

Safety Ethics
> Leaving ladder on sales floor when no one is around
> Walking pass spill as if not noticing it
> Ignoring hazards in general

3 INTERNAL THEFT
"Tell Me About A Time You Created A Loss To The Company?"

Internal loss is created by associates/employees as opposed to externals which are customers. Internal loss is the biggest margin loss that a retail store faces.

Associates Creating Loss

Although there are numerous ways of associates causing loss, these are a few ways in which they create loss:

1. Free bagging
2. Till Tapping
3. Customer Incentive Theft
4. Assisting External Theft
5. Fraudulent Returns
6. Stealing Associates/customers Belongings
7. Time Fraud
8. Keeping and Using Customer Information

How to identify internal activity?

Some ways to identify internal activity can include but are not limited to:

➢ Live observations
➢ Store reports
➢ Associate tips (Have an Open Door Culture)
➢ Physical evidence

How to respond and act to internal activity?

Responding to internal activity is important because an associate can influence others around them into taking part in the dishonest activity. Also, it is very important to act in a timely manner. In some cases, associate create losses right before quitting or during their last two weeks.

Here are some tips & guidelines when responding to an internal activity:

1. Confidentiality
2. Timing
3. Concrete proof
4. Research past
5. Live observations

Internal Interview:

When conducting an internal interview, there are three people involved. The Interviewer, Witness, and the Subject.

As a witness (most agents do not interrogate, that is your lead/LPM/Sr.), your job is to take Notes on Crucial Admissions and Subtle Body Indicators.

Internal Investigations

When it comes down to Internal Investigations, one of the most important aspects of closing out a clean case with minimal chances of repercussions and/or dropped charges is a STATEMENT of CONFESSION/APOLOGY and a signed PROMISSORY NOTE. It is important to know that special care has to be taken to get such a statement in the least pressuring and most non-chalant manner possible. This is where these two methods of interviewing come into play.

While many of you may not be certified with these methods unless you are applying to a manager position. It is important that you know what to expect when you are asked to sit in as a witness for such an interview. The following are some tips and guidelines on what to do during an internal interview:

> Most importantly, treat the incident with the utmost of confidentiality. It is important that only you, the interviewer and the internal subject know about the incidents and what will happen behind those closed doors.

> Talk to the interviewer about what the allegations are against the subject and listen to any advice that he/she may give you. This will help you gauge when to look for key physical signals.

➢ Bring in a notebook and a pen with you and be professional, this means turning OFF your cell-phone, radio, pager (pretty sure they're already extinct).

➢ Once the interview starts, do NOT interrupt the interview at all. You are not to get up and leave until asked so try and take care of any calls to nature before the interview begins.

➢ Take good notes! Write the time the interview began, how introductions were made, etc. No need to be verbatim, just brief and quick. Remember you will be allowed to go back to your notes and type them up if need be.

➢ Look for slight changes in the subject's physicality whenever the interviewer passively mentions or suggests dishonest acts that the subject has committed. Note them down immediately. These are subconscious confessions. Things to look for include, the subject shifting around in his/her chair, crossing arms &/or legs, licking lips, looking away from the interviewer, coughing, etc.

➢ Make notes of any confession and promises.

➢ There will be times when you feel like the interviewer is getting bogged down and you may have a better tactic to nail a few questions at the subject. NEVER intervene. LP/AP trained in the arts of interrogations are human beings hence mistakes happen but they are also more than qualified and trained to handle a situation on their own. You are a witness and must respect that role.

Internal left is much harder to spot than external theft. It requires a lot of time and patience, but one with large rewards. The authors have dealt with many internal cases, including one which involved 1 internal helping 2 externals shoplift.

4 PEOPLE
"The Customer Is Always Right…Yes, We're Still In Retail!"

If you thought you could do this job while hiding in a camera-room so you could avoid engaging with people, then you were wrong! LP needs to have better communication skills than any associate in the store.

How to Deal with Customers

1) Injured Customer:

- Most times LP agents have to respond to the scene of an incident and render first aid

- Whether it's simply an EAS tag that poked a customer's foot or a slip and fall , you need to treat it professionally

- The second you get the call, grab your first aid kit (if store policy allows), pen and paper

➤ Notify your Manager On Duty (MOD)

➤ Once you arrive on the scene, apply first aid and deescalate the situation. If the customer wants to have the incident reported, jot down their Name, Address, Date of Birth, and Phone number.

➤ Depending on store policy, fill out an incident form, enter it into a database, and contact your LPM/ETL/LPDR

➤ Remember, stay calm! If the situation is too chaotic or if the victim requests for paramedics, you are allowed to make that phone call. IT'S THE LAW!

2) Transients

➤ If they cause a scene, get a manager and deal with them to the best of your ability.

➤ If it gets out of hand call mall Security/ PD (always have their numbers saved on your phone)

➤ Be professional but FIRM. This is your house remember that!

➤ If need be, serve the person a documented Trespass Warning

3) Solicitors

➢ Whether it's a person soliciting for a natural disaster or just for money, they simply cannot be in the store doing so unless they have permission from the company

➢ Technically, since this is a customer service issue , try and have a manager give them the boot

➢ Make sure you watch them exit the store

4) Shoplifter

➢ It's going to be hard to keep your cool during a case which you spent hours working on (possibly on an empty stomach), but you need to keep calm with shoplifters and treat them with dignity

➢ Never cuss at them, swear or act in a threatening manner, they can easily use that in court

How to deal with Associates

Creating a professional relationship with associates can make your job easier. They are human beings, treat them like human beings. Be the example you want them to be!

1) Recognition

➢ Recognize associates for their good work

➢ If they prevent a fraud case, or you see them checking bills properly , tell them you appreciate their hard work

➢ If they respect you, they will easily listen and respond to you when you need them

2) Trust

➢ Trust with-out compromising your LP/AP presence

➢ Trust but verify

3) Communication

➢ Communicate with your associates

➢ They are the ones who interact with shoplifters/customers every day without even knowing it

➢ Teach them how to detect shoplifters, how to call them out (description, location) and make sure they know your office phone number

➢ You will catch more shoplifters if your associates are calling out potentials

➢ Teach them , Teach them, Teach them. They can't do anything for you if you don't tell them!!!!!!!

4) Sales Floor

➤ Make sure they know not to approach you when you are on the sales floor.

➤ If you are working a case and they start asking you questions, then you're done!

How to Deal with Local Law Enforcement:

Know your role. You are not Police Officers. They get offended when agents try and act like they know everything about the law.

1) How to call PD

➤ Almost every retail LP has a code word " call pizza" for PD that they use amongst themselves

➤ Before you call them , have your report ready and anything else that you will hand them over

➤ This is how you call them:
"Hi this is Jon Doe and I am calling from Denny's Loss Prevention. I made an apprehension on an adult male for shoplifting and needed to refer him over for prosecution." Then give them the address, age and name and answer any other question dispatch may have, and you're set.

➤ When they arrive, let them do their job. Collect the information you need from them, answer their questions and stay out of their way

> ➤ Knowing some basic/common penal codes will also help you better understand what the officer may be referring to:

How to Deal with Management:

Your job will be even much easier if your managers like you. In most company's the store managers will stay out of your way and will not really be too involved with your core roles.

> ➤ Know all their names

> ➤ Know their positions and which department which manager works at

> ➤ Know your District and Regional Managers

> ➤ Know their key meetings, visits and prepare

> ➤ Know, Know, And Know!

How to Deal with Neighboring Department Stores/Companies/Security Resources:

Building a good relation with neighboring departments could lead you to more apprehensions and better responses to situations where you need their assistance. It is also important to know your mall security and their limitations.

If you want to be successful at this job, take the time and effort and learn to work with people.

5 EXTERNALS
"We've Stopped Nuns and We've Stopped Bums!"

As LP/AP, Externals are your bread and butter! External theft is categorized as theft that occurs due to an "external" or supposed-customer.
Externals=shoplifters!!!

Who can be a shoplifter?
As mentioned in our saying, anyone can be a shoplifter. Every single person that steps into a store has the potential to be a shoplifter. There are ways to identify shoplifters, but keep in mind that you cannot generalize who cannot shoplift.

Two Types of Shoplifters:

1) Opportunists: These are your average "Jack & Jill" subjects. They steal on temptation and after seeing an opportunity. Most of your external cases/apprehensions (stats) will be made up of

these shoplifters. These shoplifters can become Market/ORC cases if the consistently target a store and keep getting away.

Difficulty Level: Easy to moderate; Safety Concerns: minimal

2) Organized Retail Crime (ORC): These subjects come into stores with the intent to steal and have a plan ready to go! They commit theft (& fraud) with the intent to gain sell and distribute goods at a higher profit. Some key techniques that ORC/Market Cases utilize:

Difficulty Level: Challenging (team effort); Safety Concerns: Be aware of your surroundings at all times

- ➢ Stake outs & physical surveillance of store, policies and associates (marking/defeating security)

- ➢ They almost always work in groups; get-away driver, distractions, etc.

- ➢ Multiple people hitting the store at the same time (synchronized boost)

- ➢ Boosters

- ➢ Tools and Weapons!

- ➢ Staging merchandise and setting up external theft

- ➢ Making friends within a store and exploiting that associate's resources

How it's done:

Shoplifting techniques and tactics are never stagnant! While there are many general tactics, please remember that shoplifters can be creative at times, which makes it absolutely necessary for you to always be vigilant. The following are some common shoplifting methods:

1) Concealment into personal handbags, shopping bags, backpacks, and other containers

2) Concealment on person

3) Non-concealed exit

4) Concealment into strollers and shopping-carts

5) Package/Box-stuffing

6) Boosting

7) Concealment in fitting-rooms, rest-rooms, and stock-rooms

8) Merchandise tag-switching

9) Accomplice tactics

10) Weak exits (Employee exits, fire exits, back-room exits)

How to Identify Shoplifters: Alert Signals

While everyone has the potential to be a shoplifter, there are some clear indicators which you should look out for. We call these behaviors, **Alert Signals**. Know that these are some really good reasons to continue surveillance on a suspect, but be respectful about the fact that some people shop differently than others.

➢ Antsy Body Language (shaky, sweaty, twitchy mouth, constantly looking around)

➢ Wearing out of season and occasion apparel (a long coat in summer or sunglasses in-doors)

➢ Selecting multiples of the same merchandise

➢ Selecting merchandise with minimal regard to pricing, color, and size

➢ Removing hangers off merchandise or opening of packages

➢ Avoiding high traffic areas and people

➢ Unzipped bags, empty-looking bags

➢ Multi-compartment strollers or unoccupied strollers

➢ Wearing torn and destroyed apparel or shoes and browsing through racks of similar merchandise

➢ Attempting to remove price tags, security tags, or locks

➢ Constantly entering and exiting the store, fitting-rooms, and rest-rooms

➢ Present in a high-theft department

➢ Constantly throwing glances at ceiling and/or cameras

➢ Overly friendly with associates and asking security-related questions

➢ "Cutters": suspects that immediately turn into a department upon entering the store

The Fundamentals of Floor-Ops:

"I wasn't watching you, because if I was, you wouldn't have seen me."

Surveillance cameras have played a crucial role in helping a company reduce & resolve external theft. However, preference is given to agents that can drive results without having to utilize and spin cameras all day. Most retail companies give preference to candidates capable of driving results with and without camera systems. We strongly believe that cameras are a luxury but not a necessity to be a good agent. The following tips and techniques will help you master the art of floor-ops:

1) Do not underestimate yourself (9 times out of 10, a shoplifter is too preoccupied to realize that you are watching them)

2) Do not be ashamed of thinking outside the box and doing your job

3) Avoid being in the main aisle and in the same section as the suspect (try and get a good vantage point from an adjacent department)

4) Always stay behind the subject at approximately 45° or so

5) Utilize the display racks and end-caps (use perforations in the end cap as peep holes)

6) Use props to help blend in (sales ads, shopping carts, shopping baskets, handbags, merchandise)

7) Always stay as low as possible (aisle ops)

8) Never back down! If you feel the suspect knows you are following him/her, stay at it! It's better to know what happened to the merchandise than questioning it later

9) When working with a team, remain in good communication with them via radio/cellphone but don't be a chatter-box

10) Know your price-points and merchandise (especially important if your company has a dollar threshold)

11) If you are undercover, use it! Do not be seen chatting it up with the sales-floor team. Try to have fun with it (change your hairstyle, grow a beard, dress up or down according to the general audience of your store)

Principles Leading To Apprehension

Alert Signals

1. Subject enter department, aisle, and/or section
2. Selection of merchandise
3. Concealment (100%)
4. Uninterrupted ops
5. Pass points of sale (know your points of sale)

Apprehending a subject is the epitome of your core role. You must have the capacity to make stops based on your company's policies in a responsible, safe, and legal manner. You may only consider making an apprehension (or stop) on a subject if you have all of the Principles Leading to an Apprehension covered. Be 100% sure that you are committed to make the stop before you initiate it because there is no turning back after you've made contact. There are two types of techniques on apprehending external subjects; Hands On & Hands Off.

Hands-Off Policy:

Some retailers are hands off when apprehending shoplifters. Here are some tips on apprehending shoplifters with a hands-off policy:

1. Respect
2. verbal use
3. Firm stance
4. Know exactly what they have and where it is on their person
5. Know your store limits
6. Know companies policies regarding boundaries.

Hands-On Policy:

We strongly believe that you do not need to use force most of the times. A strong presence and verbal skills during a stop are at most times all you need. However, almost every company allows the use of minimal force during a stop. It is important to know your company's policy and requirement. Do not work at a company where they allow you to be hands-on if you do not feel that you are physically capable of handling the stress that comes with it. The following tips and techniques will help you make apprehensions where force becomes necessary:

- ➢ Always identify yourself before making contact (helps avoid the "I thought I was being mugged" excuse in court)

- ➢ Use force if and ONLY if it is needed

- ➢ Approach the subject at an angle and stand at an angle to the subject at least an arm's length away with one leg slightly in front of the other (for better balance)

- ➢ If making a stop with another colleague, approach from the opposite sides and form a "V" in front of the subject

- ➢ If verbal de-escalation techniques fail you may use force.
- ➢ The key is balance. If you gain the momentum, keep it!

- ➢ Weak points to gain leverage over the subject include, the back of the knee cap, ankles and any element of surprise (having your colleague sneak up from behind)

➢ Know how to use hand-cuffs and ALWAYS double lock them. You can cause serious injury to the subject by not double-clicking the hand-cuffs

➢ Always know when to back off and have an Evade & Escape plan, (dodge an attack, push the subject away and back off)

➢ Remember your safety is more important than anything

➢ Know your company's boundaries and respect them at all times. If your company has an "Open Chase" policy, remember that you must know when to disengage

Fitting Rooms/Bathrooms

➢ Know your company's policies and protocol.

Basic/Standard procedures of dealing with fitting room cases are making sure the fitting room is clear of all merchandise, tags, and hangers. This is key as it will allow you to determine if theft has occurred.

In a situation where you ask a sales-floor associate to clear the fitting-room for you, make sure to verify every stall before the suspect enters it!

KNOW THE MERCHANDISE GOING IN WITHOUT ANY DOUBT!!!

> ➤ If possible, occupy a stall or fitting room to get the best vantage point that allows you to see who comes in and out of the fitting-room/rest-room

> ➤ Once the subject exits the fitting-room/stall, check the area thoroughly and look for any merchandise or tags that might be left behind.

> ➤ After you have determined whether theft has occurred, communicate it with your team and make the decision of whether you are making the stop or not. Be very clear!

Bathroom apprehension policies differ from retailer to retailer. Know your company's policy and procedures on this topic.

Door-Point

A significant role in Loss Prevention and Assets Protection is that of a Door Guard. A door guard plays a key role in shrink control by have a presence and can therefore be considered a theft deterrence.

Numerous companies start their agents off as door-guards in order to assess if they have the temperament to deal with pressure situations with a calm sense of mind. The following are some of the core roles of a door guard:

> ➤ Representing a line of defense or deterrence.
> ➤ Calling out suspects as they enter the store and knowing what the latest market cases/ORC subjects.

➢ Assisting with stops, solicitation, and removing unwanted subjects from the store

➢ Auditing the store and checking the basic security parameters (locks, tags, cages, etc.)

➢ Looking for any security breaches or ways to improve a condition

➢ Receipt checks and recoveries

6 SHRINKAGE CONTROL
"Lower That Shrink!"

Shrink is identified the percentage of loss of products between manufacturers and what your store has to sell.

Four major sources of inventory shrinkage in retail

1)   Employee Theft

The number one source of shrinkage for retail businesses

2)   Shoplifting

Occurs through concealment, altering or swapping price tags, or transfer from one container to another.

3)   Administrative Error

Paper-work errors make up approximately 15% of shrinkage

4) <u>Vendor Fraud</u>

Occurs when vendors create losses due to dishonesty/mistakes

Loss prevention minimizes these shrink areas through:

1) **Electronic Article of Surveillance (EAS)**

➤ These are those Alarm or ink tags that you find on merchandise at your local retail stores

➤ There is a pin that's attached to the base which if a shoplifter leaves the stores with, it shoots off an alarm.

➤ These can also come in ink tags (release ink if tampered with), and special attachment for purses and shoes

2) **Spider wraps and peg locks**

Spider wraps are used for high end electronic merchandise such as TV's, Blue-Ray players, etc. They have same the function as an EAS tags, in which if any of the wires are cut or tampered with, they release a high pitch alarm

3) **Inventory Inspection:**

Every Loss prevention Agent at any store has to examine the merchandise coming into the store. Most stores will have the LP Agent inspect the high risk/expensive merchandise coming into the stores through trucks and courier service.

4) Walk-Throughs:

A good LP Agent will consistently walk the sales floor and constantly check merchandise tags, spider wraps, or peg locks to ensure they are working properly. If there are any issues, it is your responsibility to let the associate in charge know and coach them.

7 RETIAL FRAUD
"What time does the store close today?"

Fraud is defined as a purposeful act of causing a loss to a company financially in a manner other than shoplifting.
Two Types of Fraud:

1) Credit Fraud:
This type of fraud, focuses on FINANCIAL GAIN via Credit Cards/Gift-Cards/Checks/Cash.

2) Return Fraud:
This type of fraud is induced by returning merchandise in a manner that enables the subject to gain an illegal monetary gain and impact's the company's shrink.

How it's done:

- ➤ Fake Credit Cards/Cash/Gift-Cards/Checks

- ➤ Returning stolen merchandise for store credit (store credit can be broken down to smaller amount and then cashed out!)

- ➤ Returning swapped merchandise or merchandise missing components

- ➤ Till-tap experts

How to Identify:

- ➤ Suspect makes very large purchases on multiple items (multiple TVs, Laptops, Video Game Consoles)

- ➤ Purchasing of high dollar Gift Cards with a credit card

- ➤ Someone that adds more merchandise to the tab after the first transaction went through

- ➤ Subjects that frequently return merchandise without a receipt

- ➤ Subjects that come to the store to cash out multiple gift cards

- ➤ Subjects with numerous credit cards (often using one card after the other, once one is declined)

- ➤ Hesitant on producing ID and having ID/Card/Check/Cash validated under UV Light

*Please remember that these are general rules of thumb
ways to identify & they may not be indicative of a
fraudulent situation in all given circumstances.*

How to Respond/Act:

Remember that some company's do not want you to even
respond to possible fraud, since they are insured against
fraud in general.

The following pre-steps will enable you to deal with fraud
in a more efficient manner and help deter it to a certain
extent: **(KEP)**
1) **K**now your company's policy
2) **E**ducate your sales-floor team on fraud and make alert
codes
3) **P**rovide the sales floor team with the tools and means to
identify fraud and contact you

When called into a suspected fraud incident, the following
tips and techniques will help you handle the situation with
ease:

> Remain calm and be professional-remember you
> still have not figured out whether the incident is
> fraud or not

> Validate the tender provided: Check the security
> measures on Credit Cards and Checks, use UV
> light to check IDs and cash (85% fraud can be
> identified and deterred right here)

> ➢ If something seems off (ID/Credit Card appears fake) get the details off the card and ID and move to a secluded area from where you should contact the credit card company and explain the situation

> ➢ Never say that you suspect fraud to the subject, say things like, "an approval is required."

> ➢ When the fraud is confirmed without a doubt, approach the subject and remove them from the area, inform them of the situation and ask them to leave the premises (Verbal Trespass Warning).*

*This step may differ according to company policy, i.e. some company's allow arrests on fraud, others request a partial stall tactic in order to give local law enforcement time to arrive and make the arrest.**

Follow-Up:

If your company does not want you to get involved with fraud, you can follow up with the following steps.

> ➢ Collect as much information as possible (CC numbers, ID numbers, face-shots, Vehicle plates)

> ➢ Enter the information into a designated "Fraud Category" and if need be, contact law enforcement and provide them with video and a detailed report

> ➢ Learn from your mistakes or think about what you could have done better

Remember to recognize those who helped you with the incident and coach them on their mistakes or how to improve

8 NON PRODUCTIVE INCIDENTS
"When in doubt, don't go out!"

A Non-Productive Detainment (NPD) or Non-Productive Incident (NPI) occurs when a loss prevention agent *believes* that all elements necessary to make an apprehension have been satisfied. The loss prevention agent then makes a stop and realizes the customer does not have possession of the merchandise in question. The key word here is "believes." 9/10 times NPDs/NPIs occur because a key element from the steps to make an apprehension are either ignored or missed.

What's next?

While we do believe that there is no reason why any of you will be susceptible to NPDs / NPIs, know that mistakes happen: whether that may be one made by yourself and/or your colleague. When in a situation mentioned above, it is important to apologize to the customer immediately and promptly report the incident to the manager on duty. If the customer/subject requires contact information/names you are obligated to provide them. However, NEVER ask the subject to come back into the store to "show you where the merchandise was dumped." Simply apologize for inconveniencing the subject. Never accept or proclaim an NPD/NPI.

The manager-on-duty and yourself must retrace the customer's steps and identify where the merchandise was left behind or dumped. All evidence needs to be retained and the video of the incident MUST be clipped and bookmarked. Remember, if it's not on video, the judicial system almost always takes it to be a very bad sign.

It is important to contact your Loss Prevention Manager and inform him/her of the incident that occurred if they are not present at the time of the incident. Even if the incident was not your own, it is important that he/she be promptly notified. This requires a great deal of integrity and courage, something that no class will ever teach you.

Loss prevention agents who are involved in a NPD or NPI can be minimally or severally reprimanded.

How to Avoid an NPD/NPI

It's very simple. Have <u>ALL</u> elements and have <u>NO</u> doubts.

Never attempt to watch multiple subjects at once. When you spot something that seems off the rocker, you must dedicate your entire attention span towards that subject.

You will <u>NEVER</u> have an NPD or NPI if you have obtained all the elements and have <u>ZERO</u> doubts when making an apprehension and by sticking with your company policies. They are mainly there to prevent these incidents.

It is very important to trust yourself and your teammates and to always have pristine communication. If something ever confuses you, whether that be a communication issue or a matter of trusting your colleague's judgment, let them know and fix it! Learn from EVERY stop that you make and find ways to improve them. Most importantly try and relax and have fun with your job. Someone that's more relaxed, will probably think straighter and make less mistakes.

Report Writing Tips and Techniques

Most companies require that you write a detailed account of any incident that may occur in your presence. These include but are not limited to incidents of External theft apprehensions, Known Theft Reports, Internal investigations and interviews, guest incidents, associate incidents and even damage/vandalism incidents.

It is very important to be as descriptive as possible but make an understandable and cohesive narrative. While there are several styles of writing narratives, the two styles included in this manual are the most common, simple and effective methods of writing up a standard LP/AP narrative.

9 STATISTICS & FACTS

What's the nation's most expensive crime?

Shoplifting of course!!!!!!

How much profit is lost?
More than $13 billion worth of goods are stolen from retailers each year.

> ➢ In one article it was stated that the Loss Prevention Division of Wal-Mart experiences 1 million shoplifting incidents per year.
> A Corporate Executive Officer with Wal-Mart Corporation believes that shoplifting is one of the biggest enemies of profitability in the retail business costing taxpayers 77 million dollars annually!!!!

Common Reason why people steal:
Everyone has a reason why they steal.

- ➢ To express feelings of anger, revenge, or entitlement

- ➢ To fill a sense of emptiness due to grief or loss

- ➢ To try to make life seem fair

- ➢ As a thrill or high to escape problems, numb feelings, or ease depression

Other Facts:

- ➢ Shoplifters say they are caught an average of only once in every 48 times they steal. They are turned over to the police 50 percent of the time.

- ➢ Drug addicts, who have become addicted to shoplifting, describe shoplifting as equally addicting as drugs.

- ➢ Kleptomania as defined in the psychiatric handbooks...."a recurrent failure to resist impulses to steal objects that are not needed for personal use or their monetary value."

Shoplifting Myths:

The most common myths are:

1. **If you buy something, it proves you aren't a shoplifter.**

   "I was watching older female who was rapidly selecting merchandise and had a small bag, she ended up going to the cash register and was in line to pay. Normally we would say "oh she is going to pay". But I kept watching her. As the cashier rung her up the customer motioned that she did not want to purchase (3) of the shirts and after she had purchased (2) cheaper shirts and had a bag, she told the cashier that she is going to take those shirts she didn't want back to the department. Well as she was coming down the escalator she concealed those shirts in her bag."

2. **You aren't guilty if you are just holding something for your friend who stole something in the store.**

   If you can prove this then you will be good, if not this can be risky.

3. **Acting as a lookout or blocking an employee or customer's view while your friend steals is perfectly legal or holding the bag for them while they conceal the merchandise.**

   Wrong!!! You can bust them as an accomplice. We have had cases where one is holding the bag and the other is concealing merchandise. Depending on company policy you can take them both!!

4. Most stores will just let you pay for the items you took and then let you go.

We prosecute all the time. Shoplifters will lie their way out of everything and because of that prosecute at all times if you can! Most companies have dollar amounts you have to meet before you can call PD but remember if you can do it

"I had a female adult who was cooperative the whole time, filled out information that was given to her and was one of the nicest shoplifter we have encountered. Due to the dollar amount we had to contact PD. As PD interrogated her and searched her information, we found out that every single info she had given us was false! Thanks to PD we were able to get the right info."

5. If you cry and say it was just a mistake, most stores will just let you go.

"I have had an Asian lady and Indian lady and an elderly man beg, cry and try to grab my leg to beg for forgiveness"

6. Shoplifting isn't such a big deal compared to other crimes.

California Retail stores can make apprehensions and put shoplifters under private citizen arrest. It might not be too different in other states. Once you are under arrest you are taken back and have to pay the company back through Civil Demand. The shoplifter will receive a civil ticket from sears accounting for the damage, hours the LP agents used to catch them and paper work. This will be send to their Legal department whom will sent them a ticket. If they don't pay the ticket, it will affect their credit and slowly escalate. If the shoplifter is under age the parent are held responsible for payment.

7. Being caught shoplifting can't really affect a person's future.

After civil demand, if PD is called they can also either cite, release, or take the person to jail. So now it will affect the person's future because they will have a record.

8. No one is hurt by the little bit a shoplifter takes from a store.

The company gets hurt. If the store is hands on and the shoplifter runs or fights back, the LP agent is in danger and so can other customers.

"I had caught two juvenile girls conceal cosmetics in their boots. As my partner and I stopped them and brought them back, one of the girls ran off. I waited a little and walked after her. By the time I got outside she had crossed the street and customers were telling me that a car almost ran her over as she was running. Good thing I didn't chase after her"

9. You can't go to jail for just shoplifting.

Oh Yes you can! We have sent hundreds to jail ☺

Data Collected from Compulsive no more

10 APPREHENSION SCENARIOS

Shoplifter: SH

Loss Prevention: LP

Store location will be at a made up store called John's Retail

Male stuffed a Street Fighter video game for Xbox in his pants , (1) LP agent is going to make the apprehension:

As soon as he exits , the LP Agent should already be outside waiting

LP: " Hello Sir, I work Loss Prevention at John's Retail. I need the merchandise that you have not paid for.

SH: " I don't know what you are talking about"

LP: " Sir I need the Video Game , The street fighter one for XBOX that you have stuffed in your pants.

SH: " Okay here"

SH Hands over video game to LP

Remember always retrieve merchandise first. This will
ensure you don't get an NPD. If you don't get
merchandise first and you walk them over to the office,
they could possibly dump the merchandise, and now you
have them in the office without the merchandise you are
accusing them of taking.

LP: " Now sir , I just need to follow protocol and just fill
out some papers and will kick you loose as fast as I can
because I have other stuff to do and don't have time for
something as small as this"

11 BONUS: TIPS FOR INTERVIEWING FOR LP JOBS

All of the authors have led or are currently leading leadership roles. They have complied some tips and tricks to get you through your first interview if you are new to Loss Prevention or get you through your future interviews if you would like to move to another company.

Below are some questions to prepare for in advance.

Why should we hire you?

Show your sense of responsibility, cooperation, progressiveness, and your readiness to face with challenges, which can help you to develop the company.

➢ Prepare 3 – 5 abilities that you think are necessary for your work, including: knowledge, experience, skills and qualities.

➢ Assess the importance of each ability and state from the better to worse.

➢ Do not list too many abilities, although all abilities may be related sometimes, too much information will not highlight your greatest strength.

➢ Tell them that you will protect the assets of the company!

What kind of salary are you looking for?

Provide salary scale which is acceptable for you. Or answer that: I'd like to have the salary which matches my ability. Yet I'd also like to know the salary scale for this position. Then explain that you will give the more specific number if you know work details.

➢ Possible answer: I look up to salary not to make ends meet, but to enjoy my life. I'm afraid I am not the one who only concerns about paying bills but not others. Therefore, when I look for a job, I expect a high consideration which suits my ability and goals.

How do you propose to compensate for your lack of experience?

Explain how have taken this class with us and have studied nonstop the material provided

And how can you be an asset for the company?

List the abilities that you have, show that you are capable of learning from your manager/coworkers and also from the failures and the success. Through which your abilities are increased gradually and you could surely become an expert in…

Possible answer: Communication skill, that's my most precious asset. I am capable of bringing everyone in the team together under a positive environment. My passion and enthusiasm can be of great use for companies which focus much on teamwork.

What do you know about us?

Go on the stores website, do research: products and services, sales compared in the industry, brand, management, history and culture of the company

➢ Give 2 – 3 pieces of information you know about the company, which are appeal to customers and candidates.

➢ Give out your skills, abilities, experiences and knowledge which can be suitable and developed.

➢ Ask questions about the company, such as advantages compared to the opponent firms; career development opportunity, company's ability to expand etc.

Can you describe a goal that you have achieved? What steps did you take?

In loss prevention your store will need to meet a quota. Meaning if your goal for the month is to catch 15 shoplifters you better be contributing to that goal.

 ➢ Describe a goal that you had achieved in detail.

 ➢ What was your goal and why did you set it for yourself, how did you achieve it, what were the results?

Describe the steps you have taken to make an important decision at work.

Loss prevention requires you to make important decision by yourself. For example if you whether you are sure that person has shoplifted or not could be a difference between getting fired because of an NPD or meeting your goal

 ➢ Describe a previous hard decision you had to make, what caused you to have to make it, how did you solve the issue and what resulted from it

Describe a situation in which you were able to meet a tight deadline on time. How did you prioritize your tasks and schedule?

Stores have district managers coming in your stores to check up on your teams progress

 ➢ Your answer needs to show that you are an organized person and can keep on task

 ➢ Tell them you have a calendar and have everything you need to do on that

Tell me about your ability to work under pressure?

Loss prevention is all about pressure. When you have three people shoplifting in a group and you are alone in the camera room and have to guide your partner in the sales floor. All while phones are ringing and you have to answer them, while suddenly bodily fluid is found in the fitting that you have to clean. That's a lot of pressure!

> ➤ Explain how you were under serious pressure, why you were in that positon , how you solved it and what was the result

Tell me about a time when you helped resolve a dispute between others.

You will need to bring shoplifters back into the office once you make the stop outside. Weather your store is hands on or hands off its important you are able to stay calm and convince them to return the merchandise and come back to the office without any physical altercation. If you can solve a dispute between two people you should be able to do this .

> ➤ Explain how you got involved, why you were in that position , how you solved it and what was the result

What would your previous supervisor say your strongest point is?

If you are coming from another job, make sure you talk about how great of a job it was. Talk highly of your previous supervisors and coworkers. This shows you are a respectful individual.

The other questions are going to be about testing your knowledge about Loss prevention such as

- ➤ What is an NPD

- ➤ Difference between internal and external

- ➤ CCTV, EAS , Shrink etc…

These are a few questions we have come across during the interview process. Best of luck on your interviews!

This book was intended to be a quick reference guide for current and future Loss Prevention Agents. We really hoped you enjoyed this book.

Thank you!

ABOUT THE AUTHORS

Rohullah Latif:
Rohullah Latif has worked with multiple police departments and has worked undercover with Alcohol Beverage control along with training with swat teams. Normally Agents are allowed to work 40 Hours before they catch a shoplifter, Rohullah's Hours Per Case was 7! Rohullah also holds a degree in Mechanical Engineering and is currently pursuing his Masters in Biomedical Engineering while working full time.

Hadia Bharoocha:
Hadia Bharoocha has been actively involved in serving different advisory and management roles in retail loss prevention and risk control. She boasts experience working at executive level positions with several Forbes list companies and has gathered her knowledge and training through hands on experience. Outside of of loss prevention, Hadia Bharoocha is an avid student of the biological sciences having acquired her B.S. from the University of California-Irvine and with a doctorate's in the same field being pursued

Omar Banuelos:
Omar Banuelos brings over 5 years of Loss Prevention experience. He has been involved in some of the largest cases in the history of his stores. Omar has served in many leadership roles, and is currently serving as the Loss Prevention Manager of a top Fortune 500 company.

Made in the USA
San Bernardino, CA
01 November 2015